HAVE YOU EVER...?

Other Youth Specialties books
by Les Christie

Have You Ever...?
450 Intriguing Questions
Guaranteed to Get Teenagers Talking

Unfinished Sentences:
450 Tantalizing
Statement-Starters to Get Teenagers
Talking & Thinking

Come check us out at *www.YouthSpecialties.com*!

HAVE YOU EVER...?

450 Intriguing Questions
Guaranteed to Get Teenagers Talking

Les Christie

WWW.ZONDERVAN.COM

Have You Ever...? 450 Intriguing Questions
Guaranteed to Get Teenagers Talking

Copyright © 1998 by Youth Specialties

Youth Specialties Books, 300 S. Pierce St.,
El Cajon, CA 92020, are published by Zondervan,
5300 Patterson Ave. S.E., Grand Rapids, MI 49530.

ISBN 0-310-22439-X

Unless otherwise indicated, all Scripture quotations
are taken from the *Holy Bible: New International
Version* (North American Edition). Copyright ©1973,
1978, 1984 by International Bible Society. Used by
permission of Zondervan.

Edited by Karla Yaconelli
Cover design by Proxy
Interior design by Youth Specialties

Printed in the United States of America

04 05 06 07 08 /❖ CH/ 17 16 15 14 13 12 11 10

Contents

To my delightful nephews and nieces:
Dale
Allison
Bianca
Jeff
Katie

Acknowledgments

Through their comments, ideas, suggestions, and encouragement, many have helped bring this book to its final form. I particularly want to thank the following clever people:

Laurel Hall

David Christie

Sarah Lester

Chuck Bomar

Amy Miller

Allison Hintz

Amy Bigelow

Daniel Barrett

Lisa Hulphers

Gretchen Christie

Russ Cantu

How to use
Have You Ever...?

The point behind the questions in this book is to get teenagers to take a deeper look at who they are and what they believe. Many of the questions are just plain fun, and some are even a little silly. Other questions are extremely serious, raising issues that many teenagers (and adults, for that matter) currently face.

Have fun with these questions! Change them, play with them, and add details to them—in short, use them as points of departure, and let your imagination go. The only stipulation is that the questions are not to be answered with a simple yes or no. Rather, allow the questions to be a springboard into memories, thoughts, feelings, and experiences.

Some of the questions will stretch students, some will push them out of their comfort zones, others will offer difficult choices. This book offers you and your students many opportunities to remember past incidents as well as to project yourselves into hypothetical situations. Don't be afraid of the questions. Encourage teens to reminisce, to imagine, to dream. A question can become an adventure!

A few tips:

Use this book on long drives when you a need to break the tension and get conversation going.

Code your favorite questions. For example, put **F** next to funny questions that you know will get a laugh. Write **D** next to questions that might cause your group to go deeper into conversation. Put **HT** next to hot topics that have the potential to generate heated debate.

Be wise about what questions to ask. If a student is known to get bad grades, it may be inappropriate to ask, "Have you ever gotten straight A's?" Be extremely sensitive with questions having to do with appearance. Carefully assess a question's potential impact on certain students.

Use the questions within relationships where there is a high level of trust or within small groups whose members feel comfortable expressing thoughts and feelings to each other. Encourage teens verbally to wrestle with one another over how each person arrived at his or her conclusions. It is surprising how often someone we *think* we know will respond to a question in a way that we never would have predicted. Part of the enjoyment is discovering others' journeys as they come up with their responses—especially their responses to the follow-up questions. Encourage teens to talk about the process they went through in determining their answers.

Take this book with you for a solo journey. Get away for an hour, a day, or a weekend by yourself. Find a comfortable place where you will not be disturbed and dive into the questions. You may want to record some of your thoughts to look at later or to share with a friend.

At the end of each "Have You Ever...?" question are a few follow-up questions designed to help you and your students explore the ramifications of each question. There are no wrong answers, so encourage teenagers to let their minds wander and explore all the possibilities. Before they come up with their answers, brainstorm all the possible ways to approach each question. Don't evaluate answers at this point. Merely be creative and have fun with all the options. Pose other questions, like—

- What if you had been in a different mood, place, or time? Would you have still come to the same conclusion? Why or why not?

- What if you had been with different people? How might they have affected your decision? Does the Bible have anything to say about this question?

- What would Jesus have done if he were faced with the same set of circumstances? Why?

- What would your parents have done? Why?

- What would your minister, youth minister, youth sponsors, or teachers have done? Why?

- What would Billy Graham or Mother Teresa have done? Why?

May this book bring back many pleasant memories for you and your students, and may it provide openings for you to know one another more deeply.

HAVE YOU EVER...

1
...gone swimming in a public fountain?

Why? What happened? Did you regret it later? Would you do it again?

2
...received an unexpected package in the mail?

Who sent it? Why? How did you feel?

3
...ridden on a motorcycle?

When? Where? How did you feel? Would you do it again?

4
...eaten escargot?

Why? Where? What did it taste like? Would you do it again?

...been hurt by a friend's casual remark?

How did it happen? What did you do? Did he or she know you were hurt? Was your friend sorry? How are things between you now?

...been on a mission trip?

When? Where? What did you do? How did it go? Would you do it again?

...shared your faith with a friend who didn't believe?

Who? When? Where? How did it go? How did you feel? How did your friend respond? Would you do it again? Do you wish you had done anything differently?

...scored a hole in one at golf?

When? How did it happen? Who was with you? How did you feel?

9
...been in an ambulance?
When? Why? What happened?

10
...laughed so hard that you wet your pants?
What were you laughing about? What did you do? How did you feel? Did anyone notice?

11
...thrown up on a ride at a carnival or amusement park?
Where? How did it happen? What did you do? How did you feel?

12
...stolen something?
Why? Was anyone with you? Did you get caught? What happened? How did you feel? What did you do about it?

13

...struggled through something really difficult?

What was it? What did you learn from it? Are you still going through it? How did you get through it?

14

...experienced comfort and peace of mind?

When? What caused it? Are you still experiencing it? How could you experience it again?

15

...been in a hurry to grow up?

Why? What are the advantages to growing up? What is wrong with the age you are right now?

16

...visited the Grand Canyon?

Why? Who went with you? What happened? Would you do it again?

17
...prayed in public?
When? Where? What happened? How did you feel? Would you do it again?

18
...lost your swimsuit while water skiing or diving into a pool?
Where? How did it happen? How old were you? Who was there? What did you do? How did you feel?

19
...felt so discouraged about a class at school that you just wanted to chuck it?
What made it so difficult? How did you feel? What did you do?

20
...had a dog take *you* for a walk?
What kind of dog? How did it go? How would you do it again differently?

21
...regretted something you said to your parents?
How did it happen? What did you say?
How did you feel? How did you resolve it?

22
...had surgery?
When? What for? How did you feel
before and after?

23
...wanted to change one thing about your parents?
What was it? Why did you want to change
it? Did you discuss it with them?
What happened? What has changed?

24
...wanted to change one thing about your school?
What was it? Why did you want to change
it? What have you done about it? What has
changed?

25
...wanted to change one thing about your church?
What was it? Why did you want to change it?
What have you done about it?
What has changed?

26
...wanted to change one thing about yourself?
What was it? Why did you want to change it?
What have you done about it?
What has changed?

27
...dreamed of doing something but still haven't attempted it?
What was it? What's holding you back? What small step can you take toward this dream?

28
...seen the back side of a waterfall?
Where? When? What did you see?
How did you feel?

29

...heard the ocean hitting the sand at a beach?

Where? When? What did it sound like? How did you feel?

30

...smelled bread while it's baking?

Where? When? What did it smell like? How did you feel?

31

...touched the skin of an elephant?

Where? When? Why? What did it feel like? How was the experience? Would you do it again?

32

...danced the hula?

When? Where? Describe the experience. Would you do it again?

33

...wondered why there are Braille dots on the keypad of the drive-up ATM?

34

...run in a marathon?

When? Where? Why? Describe the experience. How did you feel? Would you do it again? What would you do differently?

35

...had milk come out your nose?

When? Where? Who was there? Describe the experience. How did you feel?

36

...given money to a homeless person on a street corner?

When? Where? Why? How did you feel? Would you do it again? Under what circumstances?

37

...wondered why there are interstate highways in Hawaii?

38

...judged someone using higher or lower standards than you use for yourself?

When? Why? What happened? Did you regret it later? Would you do it differently next time? Why?

39

...thought you were going to die?

When? Where? Why? Describe the event. What brought you through it?

40

...gotten a really bad haircut?

How did it happen? What made it bad? Would you go to that hairdresser again?

41
...been to a concert?
Where? When? Who performed? Describe the event. How did you feel? Would you go again?

42
...had any compulsive habits?
What? What would trigger them? How have you dealt with them? Has anything helped?

43
...walked into the wrong bathroom?
When? Where? What happened? What did you do? How did you feel?

44
...put something in the microwave that did not belong there?
What? Why? What happened? How did you feel?

45

...publicly discovered that your zipper was open?

How did you find out? Where were you?
How did you feel? What did you do?

46

...been rescued by a lifeguard?

Where? What happened? What did you do?

47

...gotten so angry that you screamed?

What caused it? Did anyone hear you?
What happened?
How did you get it resolved?

48

...been on a blind date?

How was it arranged? Describe the
experience. Did you go out
with the person again? Would you
go on a blind date again?

49

...had a car accident that you didn't tell your parents about?

What? When? Where? Why didn't you tell?
What happened? Did you ever tell?

50

...mentally planned your own funeral?

What things would you
include (songs, speakers)?
Who would you want to be there?
How did you feel
as you thought about all this?

51

...felt really close to your family?

When? What caused you to feel close?
Why? Did you tell them?

52

...felt really distant from your family?

When? What caused you to feel distant? Why? Did you tell them? Do you still feel distant?

53

...started your own business?

When? How? Describe it. What happened? Would you do it again? How would you do it differently?

54

...invented something?

What? When? What happened?

55

...gotten beat up in a fight?

How did the fight get started? How did it end? How did you feel?

56

...had your house toilet papered?

Who did it? What happened? How did you feel? Did you seek revenge?

57

...toilet papered someone's house?

Whose house? What happened? How did you feel? Did they seek revenge?

58

...gone to a family reunion?

What happened? How did you feel? Who was there?

59

...wrestled a pig?

What happened? Where? When? Why? Would you do it again?

60
...heard your voice on tape?
What was it for? How did your voice sound to you? Why? Would you do it again?

61
...told your parents that you love them?
When? Where? Why? How did you feel? What happened?

62
...cooked a meal for family or friends?
What did you cook? What was the occasion? How did they respond? Would you do it again?

63
...had something stolen?
What happened? How did you feel? What did you do? If it happened again, what would you do? Why?

64
...understood the difference between housework and homework?

What is the difference? How did you come to understand it? Is there a difference between a house and a home? What?

65
...wanted time to go faster or slower?

Why? What were you doing at the time?

66
...fainted?

What happened? Was it in a public place? How did you feel? What happened when you came to?

67
...seen growth and change in yourself?
What changed? What caused it? What made you able to see it? How did you feel about it?

68
...had a practical joke played on you?
What was it? How did you feel? What did you do?

69
...played a practical joke on someone?
What was it? How did you feel? What did they do?

70
...felt suicidal?
When? Where? What caused it? What did you do? What happened? What brought you through it?

71

...written a letter to the President or to an elected public official?

Why? What did you write about? How did you feel? What happened?

72

...thought about how similar you are to your parents?

How are you similar?
How does that make you feel?
What are you going to do about it?

73

...thought about how different you are from your parents?

How are you different? How does that make you feel? What are you going to do about it?

74

...done something really embarrassing in front of your boyfriend/girlfriend?

What was it? What did you do next? How did you feel?

75

...experienced *déjà vu*?

Where? When? What were you doing? What did you do? How did you feel?

76

...walked into a sliding glass door?

How did it happen? What did you do? How did you feel?

77

...been on a cruise?

Who was with you? Where did you go? What happened? Would you go again? Why?

78

...thanked God for something?

What was it? Why did you thank him?
How did you feel?

79

...traveled outside of your country?

Why? Where did you go? Who was with
you? What happened?

80

...been so cold that you thought you might freeze?

Where? How cold was it? How did you
feel? What did you do?

81

...played a musical instrument?

Why? When? What instrument?
What happened?

82

...had a life-threatening illness?

What? When? How old were you?
What happened?

83

...kissed your best friend's girlfriend/boyfriend?

When? Why? How did it happen? How did
you feel? Did anyone find out? What
happened? Would you do it again?

84

...done something exciting on a dare?

Why? What was it? What happened?
How did you feel? Would you do it again?

85

...talked to someone on the phone for more than two hours?

Who? What did you talk about? Did you get
in trouble? What happened?

86

...considered what would happen if you were traveling in a vehicle going the speed of light and you turned on your headlights?

87

...dated someone of another race?

What did your parents think and feel? Your friends? What happened?

88

...traveled by train?

When? How old were you? Who was with you? Where did you go? What happened?

89

...had your name appear in a newspaper?

What for? How did you feel?

90

...had a bad case of diarrhea?

Where were you? What caused it? What happened? What did you do?

91

...tried riding a unicycle?

Why? Where? How did you learn? Would you do it again?

92

...flown in first class?

When? Who was with you? How did it happen? How did you feel?

93

...lost your keys?

How did you lose them? What did you do? Were they ever found? How did you feel?

94

...lost your wallet or purse?

How did you lose it? What did you do? Was it ever found? How did you feel?

95
...lost your luggage while traveling?
How did it get lost? What did you do?
Was it ever found? How did you feel?

96
...lost your mind?
How did you lose it? What did you do?
How did you feel?

97
...cried in front of another person?
What made you cry? Who was with you?
What happened? How did you feel?

98
...been in a parade?
When? Where? What were you doing?
How did you feel? What would you do
differently next time?

99

...stood up for something you thought was right?

What was it? When? What happened?
What would you do differently next time?

100

...been camping?

What was your most interesting
experience? Where did you sleep? What
would you do differently next time?

101

...peed in a swimming pool?

What pool? How old were you? Did any
one know? What happened?

102

...forgotten an important birthday?

Whose? How did you feel?
What did you do?

103
...gotten a tattoo?
Why? Where did you have it placed? What is it? How did it feel? What did your parents and friends say? Why?
Do you still have it? Do you still like it?

104
...had a body part pierced (other than your ears)?
Why? What part? What do you wear there? How did it feel? What did you parents and friends say? Would you do it again?

105
...tried connecting the moles and freckles on your body to spell words or make shapes?
Why? What did you spell or what shapes did you make?

106
...had someone hang up on you?
Who was it? Why did they hang up?
How did you feel? What did you do?

107
...hung up on someone?
Who was it? Why did you hang up?
How did you feel? What happened?

108
...been on TV?
What program? How did you get on?
What happened? How did you feel?

109
...appeared in a major motion picture?
What movie? How did you get chosen?
What happened? How did you feel?

110
...juggled more than three items?
How did you learn to do it?
What things can you juggle?

111
...had something published?
What did you write? How did you get it published? How did you feel? What would you do differently next time?

112
...had an exotic pet?
What pet? Why? Where did you get it?
What did it eat? Where did you keep it?
What did your parents and friends think?

113
...laughed at yourself for doing something really dumb?
What was it? Why did you do it?
What happened?
What would you do differently next time?

114
...gotten separated from your parents in a large place (like a mall or amusement park) and had your name— or your parents' names— paged over the loud speaker?
Where? How old were you? How did you
feel? How did you get separated? How did
you feel? What happened?

115

...gotten straight A's on a report card?

What grade were you in? How did you do it? How did you feel? What did your parents do?

116

...walked out of a movie because it was awful?

What was the movie? What made it so bad? Who was with you?
How did you feel?
Would you do it again?

117

...donated blood?

Why? When? How did it happen? How did you feel? Would you do it again?

118

...ordered room service in an expensive hotel?

What hotel? Where? Why were you there? What did you order? How did you feel? How was the food?

119
...wanted to be more organized?

Under what circumstances? Why? How did you try to accomplish it? Did you succeed? What does it mean to you to be well organized?

120
...eaten raw oysters?

Why? Where? When? What did they taste like? Would you do it again?

121
...looked through a telescope?

What did you see? What thoughts crossed your mind? Would you like to own one? Why?

122
...witnessed a crime?

Why were you there? What was the crime? What did you do? How did you feel?

123
...had a hero?
Who was it? What made that person a hero to you? How do you want to like that person? What steps could you take to be like him or her?

124
...had a problem too personal to discuss with others?
What made it too personal? Is there anyone you could reveal this to? Why would you trust that person with it?

125
...wallpapered a room?
What room? What style of wallpaper? How did it turn out? Would you do it again?

126
...wanted a baby brother or sister?
Why? Have you told your parents? How did they respond? How many children do you want? Why?

127
...been stung by a bee?
Where? When? What happened?

128
...rehearsed what you were going to say before you made a telephone call?
Who did you call? Why did you rehearse? How did the call go?

129
...seen a serial killer?
Where? How did you know he or she was a serial killer? How did you feel? What did you think?

130

...broken up with someone?

Why? How did you do it? What happened?
How did you feel?

131

...had someone break up with you?

How did they do it? Did they tell you why?
What happened? How did you feel?

132

...been embarrassed by your parents?

What did they do? Why? How did you feel?
What did you do?

133

...embarrassed your parents?

What did you do? Why? How did you feel?
What did they do?

134

...known someone who was struck by lightning?

Who? Where? When? What happened?
How is the person doing now?

135

...discovered that a friend was doing drugs?

How did you discover it? What did you do?
How did you feel?

136

...seen an opera?

What opera? Who did you go with? What
did you think? Would you want to see
another? Why?

137

...received a compliment?

What for? How did you feel?
How did it change you?

138
...been locked out of your house?
Describe the circumstances. How did you feel? What did you do?

139
...been so scared you thought you might die of fright?
What scared you? What did you do?

140
...recently sung a childhood song?
What song was it? What memories does that song bring back?

141
...been called by a nick-name?
What was it? How did you get it? How did you feel about it?

142

...been at a store's check-stand and discovered you did not have enough money?

What happened? How did you feel?

143

...been to an auction?

What was being auctioned off? Did you buy anything? What was it like?

144

...eaten any kind of pepper that was hot enough to make your eyes water and your nose run?

When? Why? How did you feel? What happened?

145
...walked or talked in your sleep?
How do you know? Where did you walk to or who did you talk to? How did you feel?

146
...verbally gone after some-one so hard that they cried?
What caused you to do that? How did you feel after? What happened next?

147
...disliked someone for being more successful than you?
How did you feel then?
How do you feel now?

148
...swallowed a bug?
What kind of bug? How did it happen?
Was it alive or dead?
What happened next?

149

...run away from home?

What caused you to run away?
What happened after you did it?

150

...gone out with someone when you were on the rebound from another relationship?

Describe the date. What happened to the
new relationship? Would you do it again?

151

...had a miracle happen to you?

What was it? What happened? How did
you feel? Who did you tell?

152

...walked in on your parents having sex?

When? Where? How old were you? What
happened? How did you feel?

153
...experienced a huge disappointment in life?
What was it over? How did you feel?
How did you handle it?

154
...had a huge pimple on your nose?
How did it make you feel?
What did you do?

155
...inherited anything?
What? Who from? How do you feel about
the person who died? How do you feel
about what you inherited?

156
...eaten sushi?
Why? How did it taste? Would you do it
again?

157

...had anybody argue with you about your faith?

Who? Where? When? Why? What did you do? How did you feel?

158

...dreamed in color?

What was it like? What was your dream? Did you think it meant anything? What? How did you feel?

159

...had your parents walk in on a romantic interlude between you and your boyfriend/girlfriend?

When? Where? What was going on? How did you feel? What happened next?

160

...been trapped in an elevator?

Where? Who else was with you? How did you feel? What did you do? How did you get out?

161

...wondered where the dentist goes when he leaves you alone?

162

...been on the toilet and found out too late that there was no toilet paper?

What did you do? How did you feel? Why?

163

...had your wisdom teeth pulled?

How old were you? How did you feel? How did you look afterward?

164

...said something you didn't mean just to be polite?

Who was it to? Why did you do it? How did you feel? What situation would cause you to do it again?

165
...had your tonsils removed?
How old were you? How did you feel?

166
...ridden in a limousine?
What was the occasion? Describe the limo.
What happened? How did you feel?

167
...had more than one date in a day?
Did the people you dated know? What did
you do on each date? How did you feel?
What happened? Would you do it again?
Why?

168
...been called into the principal's office?
What was it for? How did you feel?
What happened?

169
...had a unique hobby?
What was it? How did you get started? Are you still doing it? What do you like best about it?

170
...been skinny dipping?
When? Where? Who was there? How did it feel? What happened?
Would you do it again?

171
...given up watching television for a long time?
How long? Why? Was it difficult? What happened? Would you do it again? Why?

172
...set off a fire, auto, home, or office alarm?
Why? When? Where? What happened?

173
...been offered any kind of illegal substances?
What substances? What did you do? How did you feel?

174
...tried to simplify your life?
How? Why did you want to simplify it? Did you succeed? Do you have other ideas for simplifying?

175
...been caught picking your nose?
Where? When? What did you do? How did you feel?

176
...worn a wig?
What was the occasion or reason? What did it look like? How did people respond?

177

...found more than $2 in change in your couch or car?

How much? What did you do with the money?

178

...had a summer job?

Where did you work? What did you do with your paycheck? Any interesting stories about the job?

179

...had pizza with anchovies?

Describe the taste. How old were you? Would you have it again?

180

...seen someone put a wet noodle up through their nose and out their mouth?

When? Why did the person do it? What was your reaction?

181
...been to the filming of a television show?
Which one? What happened?

182
...had a best friend tell you a secret, sworn to keep it absolutely confidential, but then told it to someone else?
How old were you? Why did you tell? How did you feel? What happened to the friendship? Would you do it again?

183
...spent more time traveling in a car/van/bus, going to and from an activity, than the amount of time you spent at the activity itself?
What? Where? When? Who were you with? What was the best part of the entire outing?

184

...broken a bone in your body?

What bone? How did it happen?
Rate your pain from 1 to 100.

185

...thought about what you can count on?

What can you count on? How do you
know?

186

...accidentally killed an animal?

Where? When? What happened? How did
you feel? What did you do?

187

...tried line dancing?

Where? When? Who were you with? What
happened? How did you feel? Would you
do it again?

188
...had an unusual T-shirt design or logo?
What did it say? What did it look like?
What comments did you get?
How did you feel when you wore it?

189
...developed a friendship over the Internet?
What attracted you to this person? How did
it get started? What happened? Would you
do it again?

190
...had a favorite stuffed toy?
What was it? What made it so special?
What was its name? Do you still have it?

191
...tasted something so bad you thought you would throw up?
Where were you? What was it? What did
you do? Describe the taste. What
happened?

192

...had your parents forget your birthday?

What birthday? How did you feel? When did they realize they had forgotten? What happened?

193

...done something silly just because you felt like it?

Like what? What happened? How did you feel? Would you do it again?

194

...slept on a waterbed?

Where? How did you sleep? What did it feel like?

195

...done something really wild or dangerous?

What did you do? What happened? How did you feel? Would you do it again?

196
...worn your parents' clothes?
Whose? Why? Where? What did your parents think? What happened? How did you feel?

197
...wanted to be a different nationality?
What nationality? Why? Do you still? How do you think your parents would feel?

198
...known anyone who belonged to a cult?
What cult? What did you do or say? How did you feel about it? What happened?

199
...been degraded or humiliated by a teacher?
How did it affect you? What did you do or say? Does it affect you now? How? Would you handle it differently now? How?

200
...kissed someone before you were actually going out with them?
Who? When? Where? What happened? How did you feel at the time? How do you feel now?

201
...had something embarrassing happen to you at school?
What was it? How old were you? How did you feel?

202
...been kissing someone while you were thinking of someone else?
What were you thinking? How did you feel? What did you do?

...known someone who has won the lottery?

Who was it? How did they react
when they found out they won?
How did they spend the money?
Did it affect their family in any way?

...wondered what goes through someone's mind when they find out they just won the lottery?

What would go through your mind?
What would you do with the money?

...tried to trace your genealogy?

Any interesting ancestors? What country or
countries are in your heritage? What do you
know about those countries? What about
your ancestry do you culturally
identify with?

206
...been to a funeral?
Whose? How close were you to the person who died? What were you feeling during the funeral? Was the funeral a good or bad experience? Why?

207
...had a favorite movie?
What was it? What made it so good? How many times have you seen it? Would you watch it again?

208
...had a favorite television program?
What was it? What made it so good? Do you still watch it?

209
...deliberately lost a game you were playing?
Why? Who were you playing with? What happened? Would you do it again?

210

...had a favorite automobile?

What was it? What made it so special? Do
you still like it? Do you know anyone who
owns one?

211

...had a favorite piece
of clothing?

What is it? Why do you like it so much?
How do you feel when you wear it?

212

...had a favorite piece
of jewelry?

What is it? Where did you get it?
What makes it unique?

213

...found yourself in a big mess as a result of telling a lie?

Who did you lie to? What mess did it create? What did you do? Is it now resolved? How? Under the same circumstances, would you do anything differently?

214

...felt completely happy?

When? Where? What caused this feeling? What happened next?

215

...been to Washington, D.C.?

When? What did you see? What didn't you see? What was your favorite part of the trip and why?

216

...forgotten the combination to your school locker?

What did you do? What happened?

217
...done little things to get back at your parents?
What? Why? What emotion did you want to express? How did they react? Can you tell them now? Why or why not?

218
...been in a windmill or a lighthouse?
Where? What happened? What could you see? What would it be like to live there?

219
...bicycled over 50 miles in one day?
From where to where? How did you feel at the end of the day? What did you see? Would you do it again?

220
...met a professional athlete?
Who? Where? What did you say? What did the athlete say? How did you feel? What happened?

221
...been on an amusement park ride when it broke down?
What ride? Where? Who were you with? What happened? What did you do? How did you feel?

222
...had something stolen?
What? Where? How was it valuable? What did you do? How did you feel? Did you get it back?

223
...met an astronaut?
Who? Where? What happened? What did you learn?

224

...caught a fly ball that was hit into the stands at a professional baseball game?

Who was playing? Who hit the ball? How did you catch it? What happened? What did you do with it?

225

...flown in a helicopter?

Where? When? Where did you go? How did you feel? Would you do it again?

226

...ridden in a hot air balloon?

Where? When? Who was with you? What happened? How did you feel?

227

...been a teacher's pet?

What grade? What teacher? How did you feel about it? What did the other students say?

228

...played with toys in the bathtub?

How old were you? What would you do
with them? What toys? Do you still have
them?

229

...had to put up with a rude or obnoxious person?

Who? What did the person do?
How did you deal with him or her?
What happened?

230

...had stitches?

When? Where? Why did you need them?
How did it feel to get them?

231

...read the entire Bible?

When? How long did it take? How did you
feel? What did you like best about doing it?
Would you do it again?

232
...had a favorite daydream?
What was it? Who was in it?

233
...changed a baby's diapers?
Whose baby? What happened? Did they stay on? How did you feel about it? What would you do differently next time?

234
...saved spare change for something special?
How much did you save? Where did you keep it? What did you spend it on?

235
...sold something to a friend?
What was it? What happened?

236

...bought something from a friend?

What was it? What happened?

237

...had gum stuck in your hair?

How did it happen? How did you get it out?

238

...prayed longer than 30 minutes?

Where were you? What did you pray about? How did you feel?
Would you do it again?

239

...had a birthday wish come true?

What was the birthday? What was the wish? What happened?

240

...driven across the country?

When? Why? Who were you with?
What happened?

241

...slipped and fallen in the shower?

How old were you? How did it happen?
How did you feel? What happened next?

242

...cheated on a test?

What class? Why? How did you feel? What
happened? Would you do it again? Why?

243

...checked out your Christmas presents before Christmas?

Where were they hidden? What happened?
Did your parents find out? What happened?
Would you do it again? Why?

244
...experienced true freedom?
What were you free from? How did it feel?

245
...called a wrong number and developed a friendship with the person on the other end?
What happened? Are you still friends? Are there dangers in doing this? Why?

246
...called a wrong number and gotten a really rude person on the other end?
What did they say? How did you feel? What did you say?

247

...collected money for a charity?

What charity? How much money? How did you collect the money? How did you feel? Would you do it again?

248

...eaten so much your stomach hurt?

Where were you? What did you eat? How did you feel? What happened?

249

...wanted to be shorter or taller?

Why? What are the advantages and disadvantages to being taller or shorter?

250

...wondered why women open their mouths when applying mascara?

Why do you think they do? Do you do this?

251
...seen Niagara Falls?
Who were you with? How did you feel?
What did you see? Would you go again?

252
...seen Mt. Rushmore?
Who were you with? How did you feel?
What did you see? Would you go again?

253
...been to Yosemite?
Who were you with? How did you feel?
What did you see? Would you go again?

254
...chopped down a tree?
Where? Why? How big was the tree? How
did you cut it down? What happened next?

255
...had a perfect day?
What day? What made it perfect?
How did you feel?

256

...made a wish and held your breath through a tunnel, then had your wish come true?

What tunnel? What wish? What happened?

257

...tried to think in a foreign language?

Do you use words when you think? Images? How does your culture affect your thinking style?

258

...walked around all day with food stuck in your teeth and not known it?

How did you find out? How did you feel?

259
...had your name mentioned in a book?
What book? Why? How did you feel?

260
...caught a fish?
How? Where? How did you feel? Did you gut it? How did you feel then? Would you do it again?

261
...had a teacher question your religious beliefs?
What happened? How did you feel? What did you do?

262
...skinned a deer?
Did you kill it? How? Where? How did it feel to skin it? Would you do it again?

263
...wondered why God made us?
What do you think? Is God pleased or angry? Why? If you were God what would you do?

264
...lost your ability to laugh or cry?
What caused it? What did you do? How did you feel? What brought you out of it?

265
...yelled at a teacher?
What made you so angry? What happened? Would you do it again?

266
...envied someone enough that you wanted to trade lives with them?
Who? Why? What problems and difficulties do you think that person has?

267
...been in the back seat of a police car?
When? Why? How did it happen?
How did you feel?

268
...been caught in an ocean riptide?
What beach? What did you do? What happened? How did you feel?

269
...swallowed a goldfish?
Where? Why? How big was the goldfish?
What happened?

270
...wished you were an animal?
What animal? Why?

271
...woken up and not known where you were?
Where were you? What did you do? How did you feel?

272
...felt all alone?
When? Were you by yourself or were other people around? Describe that loneliness with a shape or color. Describe places where you feel most alone. What helps in those situations?

273
...been on an island?
What island? Who were you with? Why were you there? What happened? Would you do it again?

274
...eaten wild plants or berries?
Where? What plants and berries? Describe their taste. Would you eat them again?

275

...had a family member or friend continually borrow your clothes?

What did you want to do?
What did you do?
What would you do today?

276

...had a treasured memory?

What was the memory?
What makes it so special?

277

...wanted to die?

Why? What caused you to feel this way?
What did you do? How do you feel about it now?

278

...smelled rotten meat?

Where? Describe the smell. How did you feel? What happened?

279

...been paid to read a book?

Who paid? What book? How did that affect your reading later?

280

...hated anyone?

Who? Why? What did that person do to cause your feeling? How do you feel about that person now?

281

...had someone teach you to pray?

What did her or she say? Did it help? What did you learn?

282

...been lost in the dark?

Where? What did you do? How did you feel? What happened?

283
...wanted more out of life?
What more did you want? What would you like your life to be like overall? What will that require?

284
...smelled your own bad breath?
How did you feel? When does your breath smell the worst? What helps control your bad breath?

285
...wondered what we will do in heaven?
What does the Bible say? What would you like to do?

286
...been white-water rafting?
Where? Who were you with? What happened? What was a highlight of the trip?

287

...received a large sum of money?

From whom? For what? What happened? What did you do with the money?

288

...been golfing?

Where? Who were you with? What happened? Would you do it again?

289

...been scuba diving or snorkeling?

Where? Who were you with? What did you see? What did you like best about it? Would you do it again?

290

...witnessed the birth of a baby?

Whose baby? What did you see? What did you feel? How is your relationship with that baby today?

291
...eaten ethnic food (other than at Taco Bell)?
What was it? Where did you eat it? Why? What did it taste like? Would you eat it again?

292
...had a judgmental attitude?
When? What caused the attitude? How did it feel? Do you see things differently today?

293
...sucked helium out of a balloon?
Where? Who were you with? Why? How did you feel and how did your voice sound? Would you do it again?

294
...eaten a large pizza all by yourself?
What was the occasion? What was on the pizza? How did you feel? Would you do it again?

295
...been grounded for bad grades?
How bad were the grades? How long were you grounded? How did you feel? Did your grades improve? What would have been a better way to improve your grades?

296
...wondered what it would be like to be a parent?
What do you think it would be like? What would you do differently with your own kids than what your parents did?
Why?

297
...fed an animal with a bottle?
Where? What animal? What happened?

298
...had an enjoyable dream?
Describe it in detail. What did it symbolize to you?

299

...gone swimming with a dolphin?

Where? What happened? Did you touch it?
What did it feel like?
Would you do it again?

300

...ridden an ostrich?

Where? What happened? Would you do it again?

301

...walked along a beach in the moonlight?

Where? Who were you with? Describe the beach. Was it a pleasant experience? Why?

302

...touched a penguin?

Where? What happened? How did it feel?

303
...lived in an area that had a neighborhood bully?

What made the person a bully? What did the bully do to you? What would you do when you saw him or her?
What happened?

304
...touched a cloud?

Where? What does a cloud look like up close? What does it feel like?
What was your favorite
part of the experience?

305
...been in a car accident?

Who was driving? What happened? How were you injured? What happened to the car you were in?

...given someone a gift you would rather have kept for yourself?

What was it? How did you feel giving it away? What made it a great gift? Did you ever get the same thing for yourself?

...had someone fall in love with you?

Who? How did you feel? Were you in love with him or her? What happened?

...had friends who were a lot older than you?

What qualities did they have? What did your parents think of them? What did you learn from those friends? What did you give to the relationships?

309

...had friends who were a lot younger than you?

What qualities did they have? What did their parents think of you? What did you learn from those friends? What did you give to the relationships?

310

...driven an ATC?

Where? What did you like or dislike about it? How did you feel?

311

...taken care of twins?

What were they like? How were they different? How were they the same? What were the best and worst parts of babysitting twins?

312

...wondered why grass is green and the sky is blue?

What colors would *you* make the grass and sky? Why?

313

...tried to catch a bird?

Where? Why? Were you successful?
What happened?

314

...wanted something so badly that you behaved in a way you wouldn't normally behave?

What was it you wanted? How did you
behave? What happened? How did you
feel afterward?

315

...experienced the presence of God in a special or unusual way?

When? What happened? How did you feel?
How does it affect your life today?

316
...driven a jet ski?
Where? What did you like or dislike about it? How did you feel?

317
...surfed?
Where? What did you like or dislike about it? How did you feel?

318
...kissed any kind of animal?
What animal? Why did you kiss it? What did it do?

319
...sung in the shower?
Why did you sing? What song? How did you sound? If anyone heard you, what did they say?

320
...gone cow tipping?
Where? Who were you with? Why?
What happened? How did you feel?

321
...been ice blocking?
Where? Who were you with? What did you
like or dislike about it? How did you feel?

322
...driven without a license?
Where? Who were you with? Why? What
did your parents say? What happened?

323
...gone without food for 24 hours or more?
Why? How did you feel? What happened?

324
...run more than five miles in one day?
Why? How did you feel? Would you do it
again?

325
...wondered why people lie?
What reasons did you come up with? Are
there circumstances when it's OK to lie?

326
...wanted to go to the moon?
Why? What do you think you'd see? How
do you think you'd feel?
What would it be like?

327
...had a really awesome experience followed by a really awful experience?
What were the experiences? How did you
feel? Which helped you to grow more?
Why?

328
...looked directly into the sun too long?
When? Where? What happened?

329

...seen a comet or a shooting star?

When? Where? How did you feel?
What did it look like?

330

...thought about what you would rescue (besides people) from your home if it caught on fire?

What would you save? Why?
How would you do it?

331

...played in the mud?

When? How old were you? What was it
like? What did you like or dislike about it?

332

...slammed your finger in a door?

Where? How? What did you do?
Then what happened?

333
...stayed up all night watching movies?
Who were you with? Where? When? What did you watch? What did you like or dislike about the evening?

334
...slept in so late it was dark when you woke up?
What caused you to be so tired? What did you think when you woke up? How did you feel? Are you a morning person or a night person? Why? How do you think you got that way?

335
...stolen something from your mom or dad?
What was it? When? How did you feel? Did they ever find out? What happened?

336

...read an entire book in one day?

What was the book? Why did you read it in one day? What made it so interesting?

337

...had a family member die?

Who? How did you hear about it? What was your response? How did you feel? What would you like to tell that person today?

338

...jumped in leaves?

Where? When? How did you feel? Who were you with? What happened?

339

...asked God to give you a sign?

What kind of sign did you ask for? Why did you ask for it? What was God's response? What decision did you make after you got (or didn't get) the sign?

340
...thought about how you would like to die?

What would be the best way to die? Why?
What would be the worst? Why?

341
...gotten caught sleeping in class?

What class? What teacher?
What happened? How did you feel?

342
...spilled something on your clothes and then had to wear them all day?

What did you spill? Where? How did it happen? What did you do? How did you feel?

343
...been tickled so hard that you cried?

Where? By whom? How did you feel?
What did you do?

344
...thought about long-term goals for your life?
What are your short- and long-term goals?
How are you planning to achieve them?

345
...been in a hurricane or a tornado?
Where? When? What was it like?
What did you do? What happened?

346
...been sunburned so severely that you blistered?
Where? How did you feel? What did you put on it? What happened?

347
...been to a drive-in movie?
What did you see? Who were you with?
What did you like or dislike about the experience?

348
...had a concussion?
What happened? How did it feel?
Who was with you? What did they do?

349
...bent over and ripped the back of your pants?
Where were you? What happened? When did you realize it? What did you do? How did you feel?

350
...lost your best friend?
How did it happen? How did you feel? What did you do?

351
...been stood up for a date?
What happened? What did you do? How did you feel? Do you still run into this person? Are you still friends?

352

...stood someone up for a date?

Why? What did he or she do? What did you do? Do you still run into this person? Are you still friends?

353

...had someone forgive you for something?

How did it feel? What were you forgiven for? How did you respond? Compare and contrast it to God's forgiveness.

354

...wanted to be a cartoon character?

What character? What makes that character so special or unique?

355

...been superstitious?

About what? Are you still? How did (or does) it affect your life?

356

...wondered how lead is put inside a pencil?

How do you think it's done? Do you really care?

357

...lived in the mountains?

Where? What was it like?
Would you live there again?

358

...found a great buy at a garage sale, flea market, auction, or thrift store?

What was it? What made it so special?
How much did you pay? How did you feel?
Do you still have it?

359

...been given a family heirloom?

What was it? Who gave it to you? How do you feel about it?
Would you ever sell it? Why?

360
...restored an antique?
What was it? How did you restore it?
What made it so special? Where is it now?

361
...flown a kite at the beach?
What beach? Describe the kite. How did it
feel? What did you like or dislike about the
experience?

362
...denied knowing Jesus?
Why? What happened? How did you feel?
What did you do?

363
...wondered how
fireflies glow?
What answer did you come up with?
What do you think of when you see them?

364

...bought clothes or furniture at a Salvation Army, Goodwill, or other store that benefited a charity?

What did you buy? Why did you choose the store you did?

365

...rebuilt an engine or automobile?

What was it? What happened? Where is it now? How does it run today?

366

...not rewound a rental video?

Did you know you didn't rewind it? (Shame on you!) What happened?

367

...given up something to follow Jesus?

What did you give up? How did you feel? Would you do it again?

368

...lived by the ocean?

Where? How was it? What was it like?
Would you live there again?

369

...dyed your hair?

What color? How did you feel? What did
your parents and friends think?
Would you do it again?

370

...had a rotten smell in your room or car that you could not get rid of?

What did it smell like? What was it? What
did you do? What did you say to other
people? How did you get rid of it?

371

...had a really bad case of b.o.?

How did you know? How did you feel?
How did you get rid of it?

...thought you looked like a movie or television star?

Who? In what ways? How does it make you feel? In what ways is your personality also like his or hers?

...had your friends tell you that you look like a movie or television star?

Who? How did that make you feel? Do you agree?

...lived in the desert?

Where? How was it? What was it like? Would you live there again?

...wondered how a magician saws a woman in half?

How do you think they do it? What is the greatest trick you have seen a magician do?

376
...walked backward around your neighborhood?
What did you see? What did your neighbors think? Would you do it again?

377
...celebrated Christmas in July?
Why? What happened? Would you do it again?

378
...needed a spiritual cleaning in your life?
What is a spiritual cleaning? What areas did you clean up? How do you accomplish a spiritual cleaning?

379
...kept up your Christmas lights long after Christmas?
Why? For how long? Did you turn them on at other times of the year? When?

380
...received applause?
What was it for? How did you feel?

381
...had a friend act like one of the characters on a television show?
What friend? Which character? How is your friend similar to the TV character? Have you ever told your friend what you think? How did your friend respond?

382
...wondered how the foam gets inside a can of shaving cream?
How do you think it's done? What else have you wondered about?

383

...had cosmetic surgery (or ever considered it)?

What part of your body? Why was it (or would it be) worth it? What do you like best about your body?

384

...not been able to find something in the telephone yellow pages?

What was it? What else could it be under?

385

...felt God was calling you to a certain job or task?

How did he call you? What was the job or task? How did it make you feel? How did it turn out?

386

...questioned your beliefs?

What specifically did you question? What answers did you find? How are you feeling about your beliefs now?

387

...had a leech stuck to you?

How did it happen? How did you feel?
What did you do?

388

...sat on the grass over a sprinkler head and had the water unexpectedly come on?

Tell the story. What did you do?
How did you feel?

389

...loved someone who never knew how you felt?

How did you feel about that? What
attempts did you make at letting them
know? What happened?

390

...felt angels were watching over you?

When? What was happening at the time?
What made you sense them?

391

...thought you might have met an angel?

When? Where? Why do you think this? What did you do? What do you wish you would have done?

392

...wondered how scientists measure the size of the universe?

How big is the universe? When you look up at the stars, what do you think about?

393

...had a book change your life?

What book? How did you get it? How did the book change your life?

394

...seen a pregnant animal?

What animal? Where? What did it look like? What surprised you about it?

395

...wished you could take back something you said?

What did you say? How did you feel afterward? What did you do or say?

396

...planted a tree?

Where? How was the experience?
How is the tree doing now?

397

...wondered why the color blue is associated with baby boys and the color pink is associated with baby girls?

What colors would *you* associate with baby boys and girls? Why?

398

...wished you were the opposite sex?

When? Why? What are the advantages and disadvantages of being the opposite sex?

399

...been to Disneyland or Disney World?

When? With whom? What was your favorite ride? Why? What was the highlight of the trip?

400

...been in Boy or Girl Scouts?

For how long? How old were you? What did you like best and least about being in this organization?

401

...been in a beauty contest?

How old were you? What did you like best about the experience? What did you like least?

402

...met a famous religious leader?

Who? Where? What was your impression of the meeting? Did the meeting change anything about your perception of that person?

403
...done community service?
Where? What was the service? Why did you do it? How did you feel when you were finished?

404
...wondered why we cry at happy endings?
Why do you think we do?
What makes you cry?

405
...exaggerated or embellished a story while you were telling it?
What story? What caused you to do that? How did you feel? Would you do it again?

406

...wondered why winter-green Life Savers make sparks in the dark when you bite them?

When did you first discover this?
How did it happen? How did you feel?
Why do you think the Life Savers do this?

407

...gone to work with either of your parents?

How old were you? What does your mom
or dad do for a living? What do you
think about that job? Would you ever
want to have the same job?

408

...saved a dying bird or other animal?

What animal? Where did you find it?
What did you do? What happened?
Where is the animal now?

409
...had a friend continually be late?
How did you feel about this? What would you do or say? Did your friend ever get better at being on time? What helped?

410
...driven an expensive sports car?
Where? When? What kind of car? Tell the story. How did you feel? What did you like or dislike about the experience?

411
...stayed out all night?
Where? When? Why? What were you doing all night? What was the best part of the night? The worst?

412
...passed a class you should have failed?
What class? What did you do? Why did your teacher pass you? How did you feel about it?

413
...failed a class you should have passed?
What class? What did you do? Why did your teacher fail you? How did you feel about it?

414
...pulled a loose tooth out with string?
How old were you? How did you do it? Would you do it again?

415
...shared your faith with a teacher?
Who? When? Where? How did it go? How did you feel? How did your teacher respond? Would you do it again? Do you wish you had done anything differently?

416
...shared your faith with a relative?
Who? When? Where? How did it go? How did you feel? How did your relative respond? Would you do it again? Do you wish you had done anything differently?

417
...watched a 3-D movie?
Where? When? What movie? Describe the experience.

418
...collected bugs or butterflies?
Why? What kind? How did you catch them? What one was your favorite? How did you feel?

419
...had a place you liked to go to think?
Where was it? What made it such a good place to think? What things did you think about there?

420

...had a really humbling experience?

What happened? How did you handle it? How are you different today because of the experience?

421

...eaten frog legs?

When? Where? What did they taste like? Would you eat them again?

422

...had a place you especially liked to go shopping?

Where was it? How old were you? What made it such a good place to shop? What did you buy there?

423

...had a bad day start the moment you got out of bed?

How did you feel? What happened that day? What did you learn from the experience?

424

...driven a tractor?

Where? Was anyone with you? What was it like?

425

...seen a jumbo shrimp, an original copy, an authentic reproduction, an elevated subway, or a dry lake?

Can these things really exist? Who comes up with these descriptions? What would *you* call these things?

426
...been robbed or mugged?
What happened? What did you do?
How did you feel? What happened next?

427
...had a specific place to go where you would get your best ideas?
What place? What made it such a good
place for getting an idea?
What ideas did you get there?
Do you still go to this place?

428
... gone whale-watching?
When? Where? Who was with you?
What happened? What were the best and
worst parts of the experience?

429
...bought a car?
How old were you? What kind of car?
How were you able to buy it?
Do you still have it? What was it like the
first time you drove it?

430

...had to share a bedroom with someone?

With whom? When? What were the best and worst parts of the experience? What did you learn?

431

...ridden in an Army tank?

Where? Who was with you? What happened?

432

...wanted to be a citizen of another country?

What country? Why? What do you think it would be like to be a citizen of that country?

433

...had a place you liked to go to relax?

Where was it? What made it such a good place to relax? Do you still go there?

434
...gone deep-sea fishing?
Where? What did you catch? Did you get seasick? What happened? Would you go again? Why?

435
...panned for gold?
Where? Did you find any gold? What was the experience like?

436
...built a tree house or a fort?
Where? How did you build it? What did it look like? How did you use it?
What did you like about it?

437
...had something wrapped in your freezer and couldn't figure out what it was?
What did you do? Did you ever decide what it was? What was it? Did you eat it? What happened?

438

...been in a car when it ran out of gas?

Who was with you? What did you do? How did you feel? What happened?

439

...had your parents wear something in public that embarrassed you?

What was it? Where was it worn? What did you do or say? What happened?

440

...worn something in public that embarrassed your parents?

What was it? Where was it worn? What did your parents do or say? What happened?

441

...put up wallpaper?

In what kind of room? What happened? How did it look? Would you do it again?

442

...broken something in someone else's home?

What was it? How did it happen? Did you tell them? What happened next?

443

...thrown up at an inopportune place and moment?

When did it happen? Where were you? What made it even worse? How did you feel? What did you do?

444

...taken a shower and, by mistake, put the shower curtain outside the tub instead of inside?

What happened? Were you at home or somewhere else? What did you do?

445
…watched an egg hatch?
What kind of egg? How were you able to watch it? What was it like? How did you feel?

446
…lived in a neighborhood primarily populated by people of a different race than your own?
How did you feel? What did you learn from the experience? What were the best and worst parts of the experience?

447
…tried to communicate with people who didn't speak your language, and you didn't speak theirs?
Who? What were you trying to communicate about? How did you feel? What did you do? Were you successful? What did you learn from the experience?

448

...taught someone to do something that she or he previously didn't know how to do?

Who was the person?
What did you teach him or her?
How did you feel?
What did you learn from the experience?

449

...been away from home for a solid month or more?

Where were you?
Who were you with?
How did it feel?
What was it like to come home?
Would you do it again? Why?

...thought you could write a book like this?

Your ideas might appear in a future book!

Send your ideas to:

Les Christie
San Jose Christian College
790 South 12th St.
San Jose, CA 95112

Notes

**Write some new *Have You Ever...?*
questions of your own!**

Resources from Youth Specialties

Ideas Library
Ideas Library on CD-ROM 2.0
Administration, Publicity, & Fundraising
Camps, Retreats, Missions, & Service Ideas
Creative Meetings, Bible Lessons, & Worship Ideas
Crowd Breakers & Mixers
Discussion & Lesson Starters
Discussion & Lesson Starters 2
Drama, Skits, & Sketches
Drama, Skits, & Sketches 2
Drama, Skits, & Sketches 3
Games
Games 2
Games 3
Holiday Ideas
Special Events

Bible Curricula
Creative Bible Lessons from the Old Testament
Creative Bible Lessons in 1 & 2 Corinthians
Creative Bible Lessons in Galatians and Philippians
Creative Bible Lessons in John
Creative Bible Lessons in Romans
Creative Bible Lessons on the Life of Christ
Creative Bible Lessons in Psalms
Downloading the Bible Kit
Wild Truth Bible Lessons
Wild Truth Bible Lessons 2
Wild Truth Bible Lessons—Pictures of God
Wild Truth Bible Lessons—Pictures of God 2

Topical Curricula
Creative Junior High Programs from A to Z, Vol. 1 (A-M)
Creative Junior High Programs from A to Z, Vol. 2 (N-Z)
Girls: 10 Gutsy, God-Centered Sessions on Issues That Matter to Girls
Guys: 10 Fearless, Faith-Focused Sessions on Issues That Matter to Guys
Good Sex
Live the Life! Student Evangelism Training Kit
The Next Level Youth Leader's Kit
Roaring Lambs
So What Am I Gonna Do with My Life?
Student Leadership Training Manual
Student Underground
Talking the Walk
What Would Jesus Do? Youth Leader's Kit
Wild Truth Bible Lessons
Wild Truth Bible Lessons 2
Wild Truth Bible Lessons—Pictures of God
Wild Truth Bible Lessons—Pictures of God 2

Discussion Starters
Discussion & Lesson Starters (Ideas Library)
Discussion & Lesson Starters 2 (Ideas Library)
EdgeTV
Every Picture Tells a Story
Get 'Em Talking
Keep 'Em Talking!
High School TalkSheets—Updated!
More High School TalkSheets—Updated!
High School TalkSheets from Psalms and Proverbs—Updated!
Junior High-Middle School TalkSheets—Updated!
More Junior High-Middle School TalkSheets—Updated!
Junior High-Middle School TalkSheets from Psalms and Proverbs—Updated!
Small Group Qs
Have You Ever...?
Unfinished Sentences
What If...?
Would You Rather...?

Drama Resources
Drama, Skits, & Sketches (Ideas Library)
Drama, Skits, & Sketches 2 (Ideas Library)
Drama, Skits, & Sketches 3 (Ideas Library)
Dramatic Pauses
Spontaneous Melodramas
Spontaneous Melodramas 2
Super Sketches for Youth Ministry

Game Resources
Games (Ideas Library)
Games 2 (Ideas Library)
Games 3 (Ideas Library)
Junior High Game Nights
More Junior High Game Nights
Play It!
Screen Play CD-ROM

Additional Programming
(also see Discussion Starters)
Camps, Retreats, Missions, & Service Ideas (Ideas Library)
Creative Meetings, Bible Lessons, & Worship Ideas (Ideas Library)
Crowd Breakers & Mixers (Ideas Library)
Everyday Object Lessons
Great Fundraising Ideas for Youth Groups
More Great Fundraising Ideas for Youth Groups
Great Retreats for Youth Groups
Great Talk Outlines for Youth Ministry
Holiday Ideas (Ideas Library)
Incredible Questionnaires for Youth Ministry
Kickstarters
Memory Makers
Special Events (Ideas Library)
Videos That Teach
Videos That Teach 2
Worship Services for Youth Groups

Resources from Youth Specialties (continued)

Quick Question Books
Have You Ever...?
Small Group Qs
Unfinished Sentences
What If...?
Would You Rather...?

Videos & Video Curricula
Dynamic Communicators Workshop
EdgeTV
Live the Life! Student Evangelism Training Kit
Make 'Em Laugh!
Purpose-Driven™ Youth Ministry Training Kit
Student Underground
Understanding Your Teenager Video Curriculum
Youth Ministry outside the Lines

Especially for Junior High
Creative Junior High Programs from A to Z, Vol. 1 (A-M)
Creative Junior High Programs from A to Z, Vol. 2 (N-Z)
Junior High Game Nights
More Junior High Game Nights
Junior High-Middle School TalkSheets—Updated!
More Junior High-Middle School TalkSheets—Updated!
Junior High-Middle School TalkSheets from Psalms and Proverbs—Updated!
Wild Truth Journal for Junior Highers
Wild Truth Bible Lessons
Wild Truth Bible Lessons 2
Wild Truth Journal—Pictures of God
Wild Truth Bible Lessons—Pictures of God
Wild Truth Bible Lessons—Pictures of God 2

Student Resources
Downloading the Bible: A Rough Guide to the New Testament
Downloading the Bible: A Rough Guide to the Old Testament
Grow for It! Journal through the Scriptures
So What Am I Gonna Do with My Life?
Spiritual Challenge Journal: The Next Level
Teen Devotional Bible
What (Almost) Nobody Will Tell You about Sex
What Would Jesus Do? Spiritual Challenge Journal

Clip Art
Youth Group Activities (print)
Clip Art Library Version 2.0 (CD-ROM)

Digital Resources
Clip Art Library Version 2.0 (CD-ROM)
Great Talk Outlines for Youth Ministry
Hot Illustrations CD-ROM
Ideas Library on CD-ROM 2.0
Screen Play
Youth Ministry Management Tools

Professional Resources
Administration, Publicity, & Fundraising (Ideas Library)
Dynamic Communicators Workshop
Great Talk Outlines for Youth Ministry
Help! I'm a Junior High Youth Worker!
Help! I'm a Small-Group Leader!
Help! I'm a Sunday School Teacher!
Help! I'm an Urban Youth Worker!
Help! I'm a Volunteer Youth Worker!
Hot Illustrations for Youth Talks
More Hot Illustrations for Youth Talks
Still More Hot Illustrations for Youth Talks
Hot Illustrations for Youth Talks 4
How to Expand Your Youth Ministry
How to Speak to Youth...and Keep Them Awake at the Same Time
Junior High Ministry (Updated & Expanded)
Make 'Em Laugh!
The Ministry of Nurture
Postmodern Youth Ministry
Purpose-Driven™ Youth Ministry
Purpose-Driven™ Youth Ministry Training Kit
So That's Why I Keep Doing This!
Teaching the Bible Creatively
A Youth Ministry Crash Course
Youth Ministry Management Tools
The Youth Worker's Handbook to Family Ministry

Academic Resources
Four Views of Youth Ministry & the Church
Starting Right
Youth Ministry That Transforms